Chamber of Commerce of the State of New York

The Atlantic Cable Projectors

Painting by Daniel Huntington presented to the Chamber of Commerce of

the State of New York

Chamber of Commerce of the State of New York

The Atlantic Cable Projectors
*Painting by Daniel Huntington presented to the Chamber of Commerce of the State
of New York*

ISBN/EAN: 9783337186166

Printed in Europe, USA, Canada, Australia, Japan

Cover: Foto ©ninafisch / pixelio.de

More available books at **www.hansebooks.com**

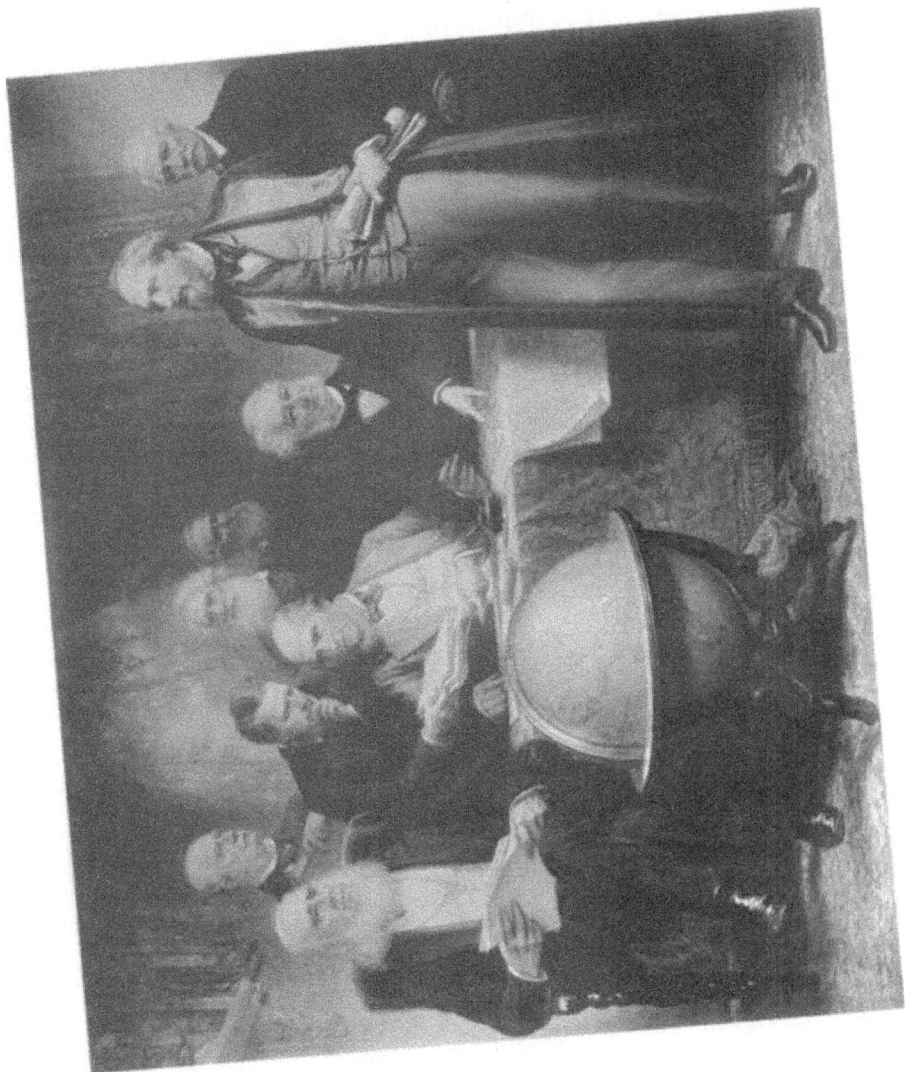

THE ATLANTIC CABLE PROJECTORS.

PAINTING BY DANIEL HUNTINGTON,

PRESENTED TO THE

CHAMBER OF COMMERCE OF THE STATE OF NEW-YORK,

MAY 23d, 1895,

By MORRIS K. JESUP, Chairman of the Committee,

AND RECEIVED BY

ALEXANDER E. ORR, President of the Chamber.

ADDRESS BY THE HON. CHAUNCEY M. DEPEW.

———————————

NEW-YORK:
PRESS OF THE CHAMBER OF COMMERCE.
——
1895.

SPECIAL COMMITTEE.

MORRIS K. JESUP,

ABRAM S. HEWITT,   WILLIAM E. DODGE.

INTRODUCTORY NOTE.

It is a matter of pride for America that the project of an Atlantic Telegraph originated on this side of the ocean. No doubt the possibility of it had occurred to many minds, but it was all a dream, until an American had the courage to strike out into the deep, with the determination to make it a reality. So fully was this recognized abroad that JOHN BRIGHT was accustomed to speak with enthusiasm of "his friend, CYRUS FIELD," as "the COLUMBUS of modern times, who had moored the New World close alongside the Old." But proud as any man must be of such praise from the Great Commoner of England to an American, no recognition could be quite so dear as that of his own countrymen. When the first cable was laid in 1858, the Chamber of Commerce elected Mr. FIELD an honorary member, and gave him a gold medal. And again, in 1866, when the final success was assured, it was celebrated by a banquet, at which the late

Mr. A. A. Low presided, and at which were present not only the merchants and bankers who compose this great commercial body, but men of distinction from different parts of the country, the Army and Navy being represented by their highest officers, General MEADE and Admiral FARRAGUT. Now the Chamber of Commerce—as the proper guardian of the name and fame of its own members—completes its gracious office of commemoration by a more permanent memorial of the Atlantic Telegraph in a historical painting of Mr. FIELD and his honored associates, that, as it hangs upon the walls of the Chamber, will remind those who come after us what manner of men they were who achieved so great a work for their country and for the world.

NEW-YORK, *May* 30, 1895.

REMARKS OF MORRIS K. JESUP, CHAIRMAN OF THE COMMITTEE.

MR. PRESIDENT AND FELLOW MEMBERS OF THE CHAMBER OF COMMERCE:

In October, 1892, the Chamber requested its Executive Committee to suggest some plan by which an appropriate and lasting memorial of the great work of Mr. CYRUS W. FIELD in the establishment of the Atlantic Cable might be preserved.

On the 6th of April following, the Executive Committee reported that after consideration of the matter, and in view of their knowledge of the long cherished desire of Mr. FIELD that the memory of the achievement should be perpetuated in the form of a great historical painting, in which the lineaments and figures of the projectors should appear, they recommend that arrangements be made with Mr. DANIEL HUNTINGTON, the distinguished artist, to execute a work of this character, to be displayed upon the walls of the Chamber.

This recommendation was unanimously adopted and a Special Committee appointed to carry it out.

Of this Committee, I had the honor of being made

Chairman, with Messrs. ABRAM S. HEWITT and WILLIAM E. DODGE, as associates.

Shortly after, a conference was had with the artist, and after hearing from him a description of the proposed work, an order was given for its execution.

Mr. HUNTINGTON at once entered upon the difficult and laborious task, and for more than a year has given it the closest attention and applied to it his best skill ; the result you now have before you.

In this connection, I beg to read a letter received from the artist a few days ago, in which he gives a brief statement of the origin of the painting.

49 EAST 20TH STREET,
May 20, 1895.

MY DEAR MR. JESUP :

The first thought of a picture representing the Projectors of the Atlantic Telegraph came from Mr. CYRUS W. FIELD. He called at my studio soon after the final and complete success of the cable of 1866, and consulted me about painting such a group. I went with him to his house on Gramercy Park, and he sent a message to Mr. PETER COOPER, who came and took the chair, as he was accustomed to preside. Mr. FIELD stood by the table, with charts and globe at hand, as he usually stood when ex-

plaining his plans. I then made sketches for the
proposed picture. Mr. ROBERTS was consulted, and
approved of the idea. Other members of the Board
differed in opinion, and there was some opposition ;
the purpose was, therefore, postponed indefinitely,
Mr. FIELD expressing great disappointment. For
many years nothing more was thought of it. In the
spring of 1892 he suffered from a severe illness, and
on one of the days of a partial rally, though so
feeble that he could scarcely walk, he called on me
and on Mr. AVERY to ask our approval, as a Committee of the Museum of Art, of his desire to present to that institution all the memorials of the
Atlantic Cable, the pictured incidents and scenes.
On that day I said to him, "It was a misfortune
that the picture he had proposed of the Cable Projectors had not been executed." to which he replied,
"Yes, it was a sad mistake, and I fear it is too late
and will never be done." I mentioned this conver-
sation to Mr. WILSON, soon after Mr. FIELD's
death, and he said at once, "I do not think it is too
late, and I hope it may yet be done." The next
thing I heard was that Mr. JESUP had brought the
subject up before the Chamber of Commerce, and
that a Committee, composed of Messrs. JESUP, DODGE
and HEWITT, had been named, under whose counsel,

authority and encouragement, I began the picture
early in the year 1894, and the result you have now
seen. I may add that I have had the advantage of
a personal acquaintance with all the persons intro-
duced, (and have painted portraits of them all,)
except Mr. CHANDLER WHITE, who died in 1856,
Mr. WILSON G. HUNT becoming a Director in his
place.

Truly yours,

D. HUNTINGTON.

MORRIS K. JESUP, Esq.

And now, Mr. President, it is my pleasing duty as
Chairman of the Committee to present to the Chamber through you this beautiful and artistic painting,
designed to commemorate a great scientific achieve
ment, the value of which we all recognize, and
which will be better appreciated by future generations. Several of the individuals whose faces are
set forth in the painting have been members of the
Chamber and familiar to us, especially Mr. FIELD,
the man who, by his courage and indomitable
energy, gave to the world that voice that now
speaks to us in silent tones, bringing together in
closer relations all the nations of the earth.

In conclusion, I beg to acknowledge the liberality
of those who enabled the Chamber to become the

possessor of this great work of art, and to express
to them its appreciation and thanks.

Mr. JESUP read the following letter from Mr.
Justice FIELD, of the United States Supreme Court:

SUPREME COURT OF THE UNITED STATES,
WASHINGTON, D. C.,
May 20th, 1895.

To the Chamber of Commerce of New-York:

GENTLEMEN: I have to acknowledge your kind
invitation to be present at the unveiling of the
painting of the Projectors of the Atlantic Cable.
Few subjects are more worthy of the genius of
the artist or the historian. When COLUMBUS discovered the New World, it was almost as far
away from the Old World as if it had been in
another planet. Improvements in the art of naviga-
tion brought the continents nearer to each other;
but it was reserved to modern science to make it
possible to have instantaneous communication.
The mere conception was almost a Divine inspira-
tion, but to carry it into execution was the work of
twelve laborious years—years interrupted by defeats
and disappointments, that would have broken down
the courage of most men. All this I had reason to

know from my relation to one who took such a part in the enterprise, and hence, I should be with you on an occasion of so much interest, but that it comes in the very last week of the Court. You need, however, no individual presence. The great painting before you speaks for itself. The faces there portrayed are familiar to the people of New-York as among those of their most honored citizens. All of them are now gone from the world, but the remembrance of what they did may well be a matter of pride to their children, and it is fitting that this historic scene should be put on canvas by your distinguished artist, and placed in the great hall of your Chamber of Commerce, to preserve the memory of it to future generations.

I am, with great respect,

Yours very sincerely,

STEPHEN J. FIELD.

ADDRESS BY THE HON. CHAUNCEY M. DEPEW.

MR. PRESIDENT AND GENTLEMEN: The picture which is hung to-day upon the walls of the Chamber of Commerce illustrates one of the great events of history. The men who are portrayed in it are representative of American pluck and opportunity. Each of them, in his own way, did much for the commercial greatness of the metropolis and the grandeur of the commerce of our country. They were, in the broadest and best sense, self-made men. They were not accidents, but architects. They commenced life without fortune or influence, with no other capital than character and brains, and won power, fame and fortune.

The conditions attendant upon the acquisition of wealth dry up generous impulses and make the possessors hard, cold and unsympathetic. The notable exceptions to the rule are the more deserving of admiration and praise. These six New-Yorkers and Americans had never permitted their failures or their successes to dim their enthusiasm or dull their imagination. Though the most practical of business men, yet they could risk their money and their reputations upon a scheme which, in its beginnings, had little else to recommend it but patriotism and humanity.

Those who win great wealth suddenly or fortuitously, risk it with a recklessness born of the ease with which it came. But they who have slowly and laboriously climbed the ladder of fortune, look with suspicion upon enterprises, the opportunities of which have not been thoroughly tested and tried. They know that, with their experience and demonstrated ability, they can outstrip their fellows and secure success where less able but more adventurous travelers have beaten the path and shown the way.

The six gentlemen who gathered in CYRUS W. FIELD's parlor on March 10th, 1854, were splendid examples of American success. CYRUS FIELD, the son of a Connecticut clergyman who had naught to give his family but an education and an example, had retired from business with a fortune at thirty-five. His brother, DAVID DUDLEY, stood in the front rank of American lawyers, his codifications of law having secured national and international recognition. MARSHALL O. ROBERTS had ventured with equal success upon the ocean and upon the land. WILSON G. HUNT was a conservative, broad-minded and eminently successful New-York merchant. MOSES

TAYLOR was one of the most far-sighted and eminent bankers and projectors of America. PETER COOPER had overcome almost insurmountable obstacles in his career, and at ninety years of age was still quick in his sympathy with the growth of the City, the development of his country, with the needs of mankind and with every effort for the education and assistance of youth.

Before this assemblage Mr. FIELD placed the project of an Atlantic cable. The wire which could be successfully laid under the ocean had not yet been invented or manufactured. The possibilities of the construction of such a line had not been tested. The perils and obstacles between Europe and America and in the depths of ocean were unknown. The factors presented to these men of caution and of sense were, a letter from Lieut. MAURY, of the United States Navy, expressing a belief in a level plateau under the ocean between Newfoundland and Ireland; a letter from Prof. MORSE, then radiant with the young fame of his successful telegraph, saying that though it never had been tried, he yet believed a message could be transmitted through three thousand miles of wire; and the enthusiasm and confidence of CYRUS W. FIELD. "It will unite the Old World and the New, it will promote peace

and civilization, it will help commerce, it will bring
our country in contact with the world, and upon that
I will stake my reputation, my undivided time and
energies and my fortune," said Mr. FIELD. "This is
more patriotism than business," was the answer of
his guests, "but we will furnish the money required."

Before the laying of the cable could be commenced
the wires must be put under the Gulf of St.
Lawrence and stretched through four hundred miles
of unbroken wilderness which had never been
traversed by man, across Newfoundland to St. Johns.
As if upon a holiday excursion, the party sailed
from New-York, to lose their line in the Gulf
of St. Lawrence, and returned chastened and
dispirited. Again Mr. FIELD set forth, this time to
complete his enterprise to the point where the connection could be made with the expected cable from
Europe. He went abroad as a missionary in 1856,
preaching the cable and its opportunities to English
statesmen and bankers. There was no need of his
arguing its value; that was thoroughly understood
on both sides of the Atlantic. The fleet was
gathered. It left the coast of Ireland with its
precious burden, speeded by cheers and salutes and
guns, to have the line break when three hundred

miles from the shore. Undaunted, undismayed,
nerved with new energy by defeat, made of the stuff
with which the world's conquerors have been en-
dowed, CYRUS FIELD appealed once more to falter-
ing friends on both sides of the water. Once more
they responded. The United States and Great
Britain contributed the best frigates of their navies,
which sailed in company to mid-ocean, where, as a
sign of the amity and concord which was to follow
success, the American man of war steamed with her
freight of coil toward the Emerald Isle, and the
British man of war, with her half of it, toward
America. Hundreds of miles of wire had found a
bed at the bottom of the ocean and been successfully tested, when the storms of the sea broke the
cable, and the expedition returned to England.

The indomitable pluck found in the Puritan strain
spurred dying hope to one last effort, and the
cable was laid. President BUCHANAN sent his message to Queen VICTORIA, and the Queen responded
with equal cordiality and gratitude. The world was
aflame with eager expectation and joy. The builder
came to our City a conqueror, to be welcomed with
ovations and a triumph as significant, as grand and
as national, as any which ever hailed a CÆSAR, with
the world at his chariot wheels, entering imperial

Rome. The messages continued to fly back and
forth. Then came the dramatic and tragic end.
There were no hecatombs of dead, no wailing of
wounded, no bereaved homes, but there was a
wreck and destruction of hope involving more
people and more countries than resulted from any
other disaster of the ages. While the guns were
booming, the torchlights flashing, and the rockets
bursting in air, on that very night the cable of 1858
ceased to work. The first shock over, the mad-
dened populace, looking as ever for a victim, pursued the victor of yesterday as the fraud of the
morrow. Torrents of invective and of epithet from
the press, the exchanges and the public were
poured upon the scheme and its author. "The
cable had never worked ; the messages were all
false ; we have been tricked and deceived for stock-
jobbing purposes," was the popular cry. To add to
the troubles of the City's defeated and discredited
guest, the financial cyclone which was then sweep-
ing the country scattered his fortune.

Few strains in the blood of the human race, except
that of CROMWELL and his IRONSIDES, of BREWSTER
and CARVER, and their companions, who had framed
the great charter of liberty in the cabin of the May-
flower, could have survived this trial, humiliation

and disaster. But CYRUS FIELD arose from the
wreck of his fortune, his hopes and his reputation,
with sturdier faith and sterner purpose. Forty
times he crossed the seas. Congresses and Parlia-
ments, the Cabinets of Presidents and the Ministers
of the Queen, boards of trade and chambers of commerce, the parlors of bankers and the directors'
rooms of banks, the libraries of scientists and the
moss-grown halls of ancient universities, became
familiar with this intrepid and irrepressible enthu-
siast. For eight long years he pursued his quest,
exhibited his maps, submitted his tests, formulated
his calculations and addressed his appeals. There
is no human power which can resist the assaults of a
man of genius, energy and irrevocable purpose, who
believes that he is right and is battling for a great
cause. The great powers of the world, government
and finance, surrendered to CYRUS FIELD in 1866.

The adventures and alarms, the machinery broken
and repaired, the alternate hopes and despair, the
forces of nature in the Atlantic working their
mightiest against the domination of the skill, the
invention, the will and the genius of man on the
Great Eastern during the three weeks while the
cable was paying out from her stern, and on either
side of the ocean nations awaiting the result, pre-

sented a picture unequalled in all the marvellous stories which have aroused the eloquence, the poetry and the painting of the centuries in the marches and battles of history.

When I was in Genoa, a year ago, looking upon that splendid statue of COLUMBUS, which is its chief monument, I noticed upon the base this inscription: "There was one world. He said, 'let there be two,' and there were two." After four centuries Mr. FIELD, with his cable, had reunited the two worlds, and in gladness and peace the earth was one.

The first message on MORSE's telegraph was the exclamation of wonder and thanksgiving: "What hath God wrought." The aspiration of the nations, breathed simultaneously at the eastern and the western ends of the Atlantic cable, was "Glory to God on high, and on earth peace and good will among men."

A happy commentary upon the far reaching influence and ultimate results of this quick communication between America and Europe was found among the first of the messages which flashed across the wire. This was the announcement of the agreement to submit the Alabama claims to arbitration. It was the beginning of that movement for the peace of the world by which the disputes of nations shall be settled, not by the arbitrament of arms, but by the calm procedure of judicial tribunals. No power can estimate and no language adequately state the benefits derived from the Atlantic Cable, and the others which have been subsequently laid, by the United States and by the Old World. Commerce has been revolutionized, inter-communication between the different parts of the earth quickened, and universal intelligence disseminated. The people have been benefited in cheaper living, better homes, higher thinking and broader education ; peace has been promoted among nations, and the American Republic has taken its place among the governments of the world, to both maintain the position in which WASHINGTON placed it of non-interference in the politics of other continents, and to enforce by the stern application of the MONROE doctrine, non-interference by the governments of other continents in the politics or the governments of the Americas. Upon Great Britain and the United States, the mother country and the great Republic, the result has been such constant and instantaneous communication, such close and intimate relations, such a volume of commercial exchanges, such an interchange of peoples and of ideas, that while disputes will be impossible to avoid and differences must continually arise, they will always be settled with peace and honor.

The story of nations is contained in multitudes of volumes and fills libraries, but a few providential and marvellous events have sown the seeds of history. In a lifetime of earnest study one could hardly grasp the details of the rise and fall of dynasties and kingdoms, of races and peoples, of politics and parties, of invention and discovery, and of philosophies and religions. In a broad generalization the wonderful development of modern times can be traced to three eras—the Crusades, the discovery of America and the laying of the Atlantic Cable.

Last Sunday was celebrated at Clèrmont, in France, the eight hundredth anniversary of the preaching of the sermon by PETER the Hermit, which led to the first Crusade. Europe was then groaning under the iron heel of the feudal system. There was no law but the despotic will of the petry baron, and no protection against his exactions and the outrages of his army of retainers. The Church offered refuge, but it was not strong enough to protect the weak and the many against the armed might of the few. A pall of ignorance and of superstition rested upon the western world. This inspired priest moved alike princes and people to a supreme effort for the rescue of the holy sepulchre from the grasp of the infidel. The Crusades broke the strength of the barons, increased the authority of both the Church and the State, and brought about that concentration of power which made possible constitutional government and parliamentary liberty. They opened the way for Runnymede, for Magna Charta, for the Bill of Rights and for the Declaration of Independence. The East had all the culture of the world. It had all the literature, the arts and the sciences, which existed in that age. It possessed organized commerce and enlightened merchants. The contact of brute force from Europe with this higher civilization cultivated the paladin and the palmer, and brought back to Europe a revival of literature, an impulse for trade, and an ambition for invention and discovery. The Crusades founded the universities which gave to the middle age its scholars and philosophers. They brought out from the libraries the hidden treasures of the ancient world, and through the Greek and Latin authors made possible the names whose works are part of the treasures of mankind. To them and their results can be traced the telescope, the microscope, the compass, and crowning them all in its beneficent influences, the printing press. It required four hundred years to accomplish these results and bring Europe up to this standard.

Then COLUMBUS wandered from court to court, pressing upon royal and unwilling ears his belief in a Western hemisphere. Others had discovered this continent, but the times were not ripe for the announcement or the appreciation of the fact. In the fullness of preparation the imperious and resistless COLUMBUS compelled audience for his scheme and fleets for his adventure. The discovery of the New World became the most important chapter in the history of the human race. Far beyond its material advantages in affording homes for the crowded populations of the Old World, were the opportunities which it gave for the development and practice of civil and religious liberty. Under the benign and wonder working influences of these principles, this Republic has flowered and flourished as the home of the oppressed, as the land of the free, as the exemplar of man's opportunities for governing himself, and as a disseminator of the value and possibility of liberty around the globe.

The United States of 1854, when these gentlemen met, were as distinct from the United States of to-day as 1854 was distant from the time of the Revolutionary War. They were isolated from

Europe by the trackless ocean, and separated by an eight days' journey from its shores. This infrequent and difficult contact with the world promoted provincialism and protected slavery in our Republic. We were not ready for instantaneous communication with the Old World to preach by lightning from day to day the lessons of our liberty so long as under our Constitution and laws four millions of human beings were held in bondage. When the cable was projected all parties in the United States were discussing, not whether slavery should be abolished, not whether the stigma should be removed, not whether the curse should be obliterated, but whether it should be extended over virgin territories. All parties were agreed that it should be protected by the power of the Government where it already existed. In the eight years following the failure of the cable of 1858 the civil war had both devastated and purified the land. Slavery was gone, the Republic was free, and the principles of the Declaration of Independence were the fundamental law of the country. The regenerated and disenthralled Republic, with the stars of its flag undimmed, was prepared by example and theory to give to people suffering under oppression everywhere, sympathy, encouragement and moral help.

Thus while four hundred years after the Crusades

had enlightened Europe, COLUMBUS discovered America, so four hundred years after COLUMBUS set up his banner on San Salvador the Atlantic cable united our country in instantaneous communication with every part of the earth. For the gratification of our national pride, and for the recognition of our prestige and power, we were happily prepared for this daily review of our development and progress.

The six gentlemen who met in the little library in Gramercy Park forty years ago have all joined the majority beyond the grave. There was no publicity given to their gathering, and the results of their evening conference failed to attract the attention of the Argus-eyed press. But the States General of Holland, staking the resources of their country upon the issue of religious liberty ; the barons at Runny-mede, forcing from the throne, with their swords, the principles of civil liberty ; the Continental Congress, formulating the measures which should dedicate a continent to the equality of all men before the law ; neither, nor all of them, accomplished any greater results for mankind than those which will flow in future ages from the success of the enterprise started so courageously by the gentlemen whose portraits will henceforth, upon yonder historical canvas, adorn the walls of this venerable Chamber.

REPLY OF ALEXANDER E. ORR, PRESIDENT OF THE CHAMBER.

LADIES AND GENTLEMEN : I think we are all of one mind that the Chamber of Commerce is unusually favored this afternoon, not only as the recipient of a superb historic painting, commemorative of a great scientific and commercial achievement, but also in having it presented in language that is akin to a beautifully conceived epic poem. I am sure that the words which Mr. JESUP and Doctor DEPEW have so charmingly spoken to us have found a permanent abiding place in all our hearts.

You may remember, perhaps, the story that has been told of a compositor who, when setting the type of SHAKESPEARE's play of HAMLET, came to that place in the manuscript where the hero is made to moralize after this fashion :

> " There are books in the running brooks,
> Sermons in stones, and good in every thing."

The compositor paused, and critically glanced a second time at the text. " Why, no," he said, " there is surely something wrong here. Whoever

heard of 'sermons in stones' and 'books in brooks;'
the author must have been sadly mixed when he
wrote these lines, but I shall set him right ; I will
put the sermons back into the books and the stones
into the brooks, where they properly belong, and
then all will be well," and so he set the type to
read :

> " There are stones in the running brooks,
> " Sermons in books, and good in every thing."

The compositor was altogether too practical, and
lacked imagination. He had yet to learn that the
great book of nature is the immediate handiwork of
the Almighty, and that to the thoughtful, the con-
templative and the Christian man, the rocks and
mountains, the hills and valleys, the rivers and
streamlets, the trees and flowers, speak with an
eloquence superior to that of sermons that may be
found in books or preached from the most intellec-
tual pulpits.

And so this picture will be a continuous inspira-
tion of encouragement for all time to come to those
who look upon it and study its story of faith, and
hope, and perseverance, and patience, and courage,
and philanthropic purpose, and genuine and loyal
friendships in the crucial time of need, and of

abiding confidence in scientific research and commercial enterprise, as a means of overcoming what may appear at first sight to be insuperable obstacles in the pathway of the world's advancement.

Many thoughts have been suggested by the eloquent words of Mr. JESUP and Doctor DEPEW that deserve our serious consideration, but it seems to me the one that is now most prominent to the commercial mind, is the intimate relationship that exists between science and commerce, and the mutual benefits that each enjoys as a result of this close compact. Science is encouraged and stimulated to further and more comprehensive research, because commerce promptly adapts to her own uses those wonderful discoveries that overcome the drawbacks of time and space and the many other hinderances that have heretofore stood in the way of her more rapid and successful development. Commerce is exceedingly appreciative and generous, and in these times of intense commercial activity, science is made to understand that for all her discoveries that can be commercially utilized, there awaits a liberal commercial value, and hence the present age is one of remarkable energy in the line of scientific invention.

What new fields the scientist of the coming

generation will open up, and what new appliances will be offered to the commerce of the future it is absolutely impossible for us to determine, but this we do know, however, that the college student (indeed, I might almost say, the school boy) of to-day, holds as household words the scientific mysteries of yesterday, and so it will ever be, till knowledge culminates, and "we shall know even as we are known;" and when that time comes, science, which is now sometimes prone to stray from "the straight and narrow path" into the realms of scepticism, will be found to be in line with the gospel of the great and glorified Redeemer of Calvary, because "the earth shall (then) be full of the knowledge of the Lord, as the waters cover the sea."

Mr. JESUP and Doctor DEPEW, in the name of and on behalf of the Chamber of Commerce of the State of New-York, I accept, with pleasure and pride, and thankfulness this magnificent historic picture. We shall esteem it the masterpiece of our art collection, and when we come to possess our own building, which I trust we shall, at no very distant period, we will honor it, and we shall honor ourselves by giving to it the place of honor on our walls.

Mr. JESUP, as Chairman of the Committee, which

has so admirably fulfilled its mission, will you kindly grant us the further favor of conveying to the donors of this most beautiful gift, assurances of the fullness of our appreciation, our gratitude, and our thanks.

DESCRIPTION OF THE PAINTING.

The painting represents a meeting of the Atlantic Cable Projectors at the residence of Mr. CYRUS W. FIELD on Gramercy Park. Mr. PETER COOPER is presiding. Mr. FIELD is calling attention to a chart of Trinity Bay, pointing to Heart's Content as a safe harbor for landing the cable. Mr. DAVID DUDLEY FIELD stands by the President with a law book. Mr. CHANDLER WHITE is handing estimates of expense to Mr. MARSHALL O. ROBERTS; next to whom, at the table, is Mr. MOSES TAYLOR, listening to Mr. FIELD'S argument; near whom, at the end of the table, stands Mr. WILSON G. HUNT, who, though he joined them some time after their first organization, remained a staunch supporter of the project to the end. Prof. SAMUEL F. B. MORSE, the Electrician of the Company, is standing behind Mr. ROBERTS, and by his side Mr. DANIEL HUNTINGTON, the artist, sketching.

The size of the canvas is seven feet three inches by nine feet.

DONORS OF THE PAINTING.

The ESTATE OF PETER COOPER, by ABRAM S. HEWITT, Executor.

The ESTATE OF WILSON G. HUNT, by EDWARD T. HUNT and ELLEN D. HUNT.

MORRIS K. JESUP.

Miss MARY M. ROBERTS.

GEORGE J. GOULD.

THE WESTERN UNION TELEGRAPH COMPANY, by THOMAS T. ECKERT, President.

J. PIERPONT MORGAN.

JOHN T. TERRY.

EDWIN GOULD.

Mrs. MELISSA P. DODGE.

WILLIAM E. DODGE.

D. WILLIS JAMES.

SAMUEL D. BABCOCK.

JAMES M. CONSTABLE.

CORNELIUS VANDERBILT.

Mrs. PERCY R. PYNE.

GEORGE C. TAYLOR.

Mrs. Robert Winthrop.

Mrs. George Lewis, Jr.

Henry A. C. Taylor.

F. Frederic Gunther.

Kuhn, Loeb & Co.

Cornelius N. Bliss.

Charles A. Hoyt.

Hugh N. Camp.

William H. Webb.

Henry Hentz.

Alexander E. Orr.

George Bliss.

John Crosby Brown.

James McCreery.

John Claflin.

Charles Lanier.

James Speyer.

John Sloane.   .

James A. Hearn & Son.

James W. Pinchot.

R. H. Macy & Co.

Charles L. Tiffany.

H. C. Fahnestock.

John L. Riker.

Malcolm Graham.

D. O. Mills.

A. A. Low.

W. Bayard Cutting.

C. P. Huntington.

John D. Crimmins.

John D. Jones.

Isaac Stern.

Richard T. Wilson.

Charles Butler.

John S. Kennedy.

www.ingramcontent.com/pod-product-compliance
Lightning Source LLC
Chambersburg PA
CBHW021453090426
42739CB00009B/1736